Hello!
I am a lion.

I0115147

Lions are found in Africa and a small part of India.

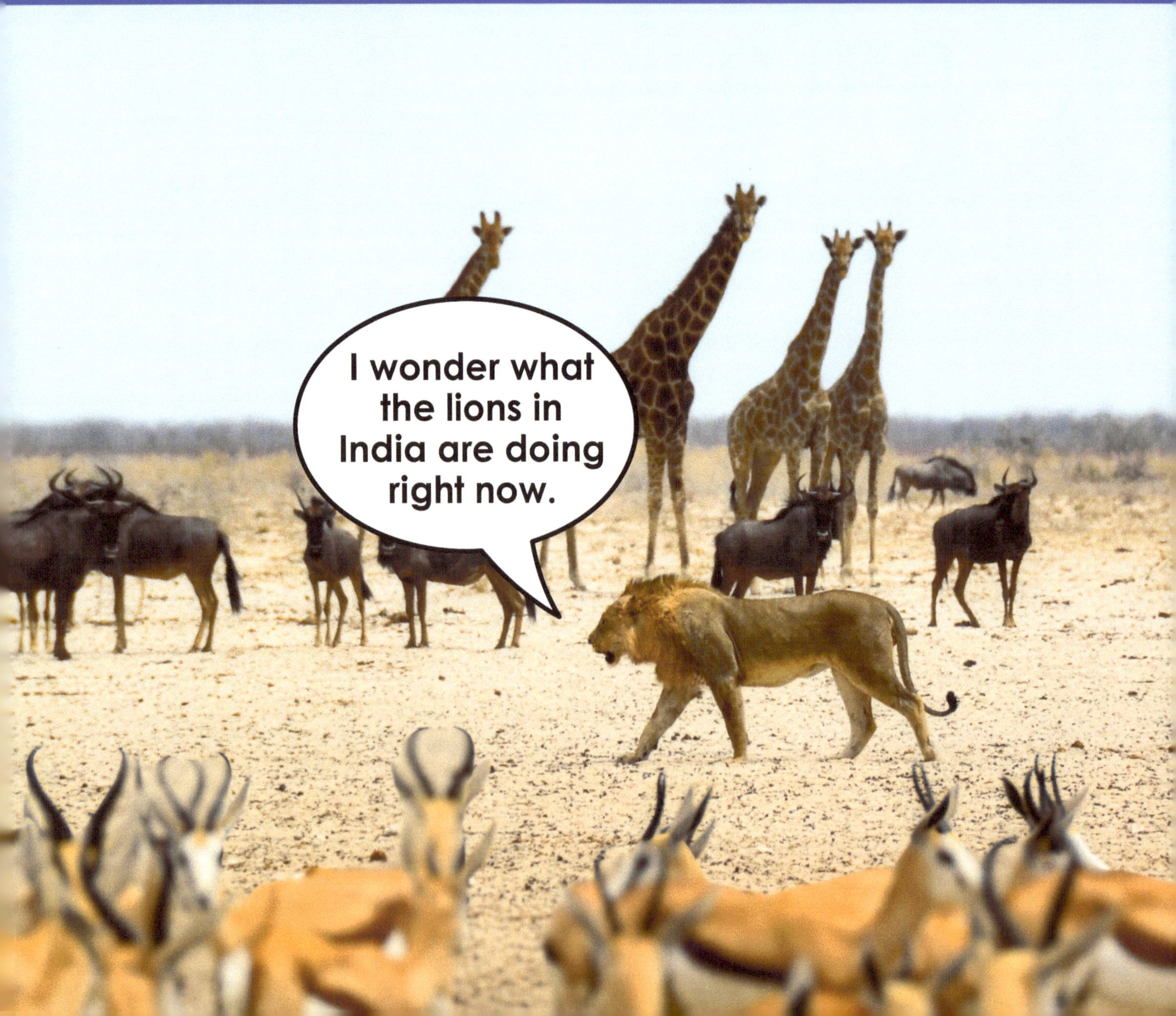

Please call me *Mr. Lion*.

The scientific name for lions is "Panthera leo".

The average lifespan of a lion in the wild is around 8-15 years.

The mane of a male lion gets darker as he gets older.

Lions are protective of their home.

Lions are known as the "King of the Jungle".

I will rub my face against trees and rocks so others know this is my place!

Lions also mark their territory by spraying urine to leave a scent.

Adult male lions weigh between 330 - 550 lbs. (150 - 250 km).

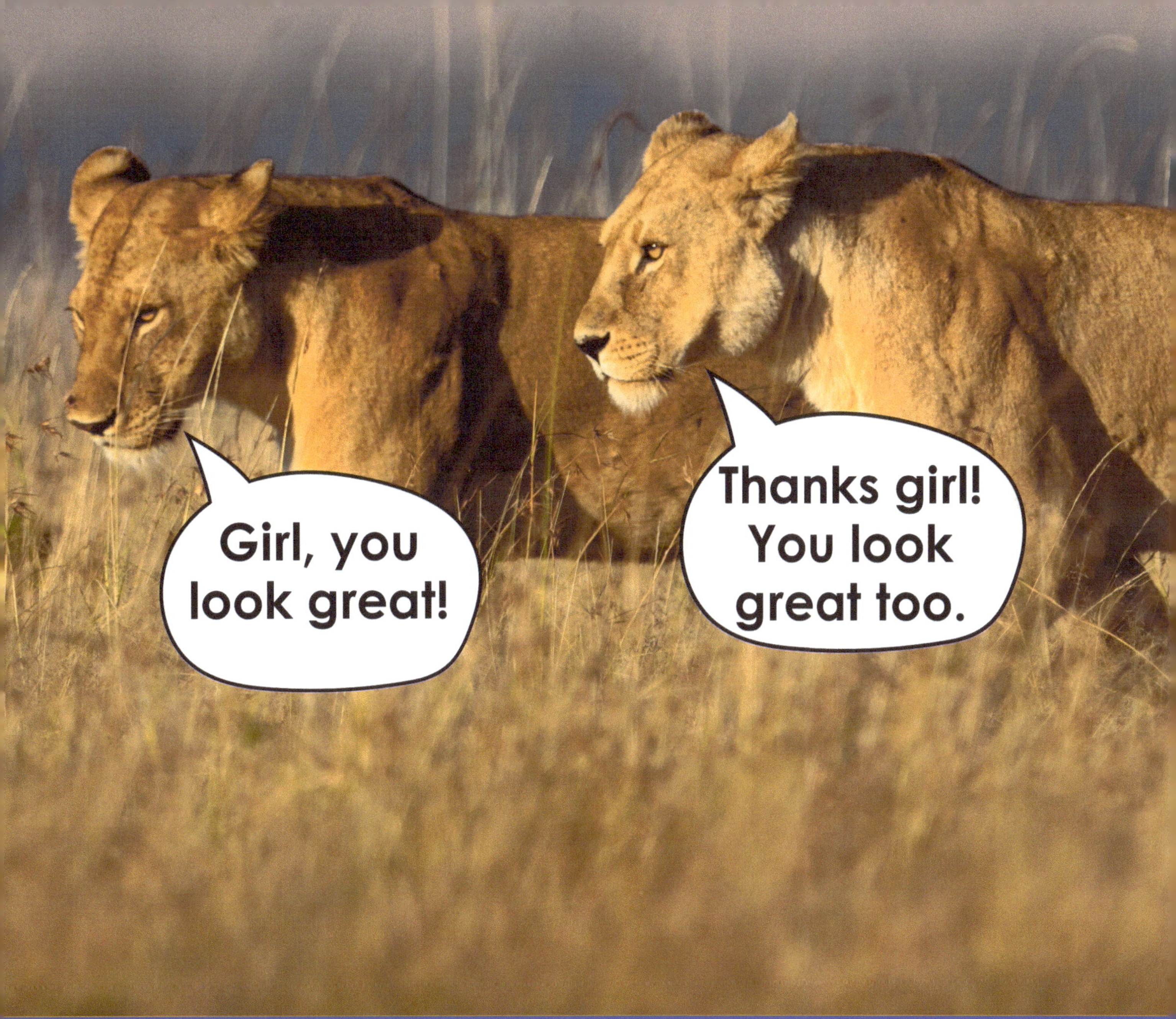

Adult female lions, weigh between 260 - 400 lbs. (120 -180 kg).

Female lions don't have manes.

Female lions are called "lionesses".

We have our own special hairstyle.

Male lions have a big, fluffy mane of hair around their necks that makes them look like they have a golden crown.

Lions are "crepuscular". This means they are most active during dawn and dusk.

Lions sleep a lot, and they can sleep for up to 20 hours a day!

Lions are "carnivores", which means they eat meat.

I'm already thinking about having seconds.

Lions have a great sense of smell.

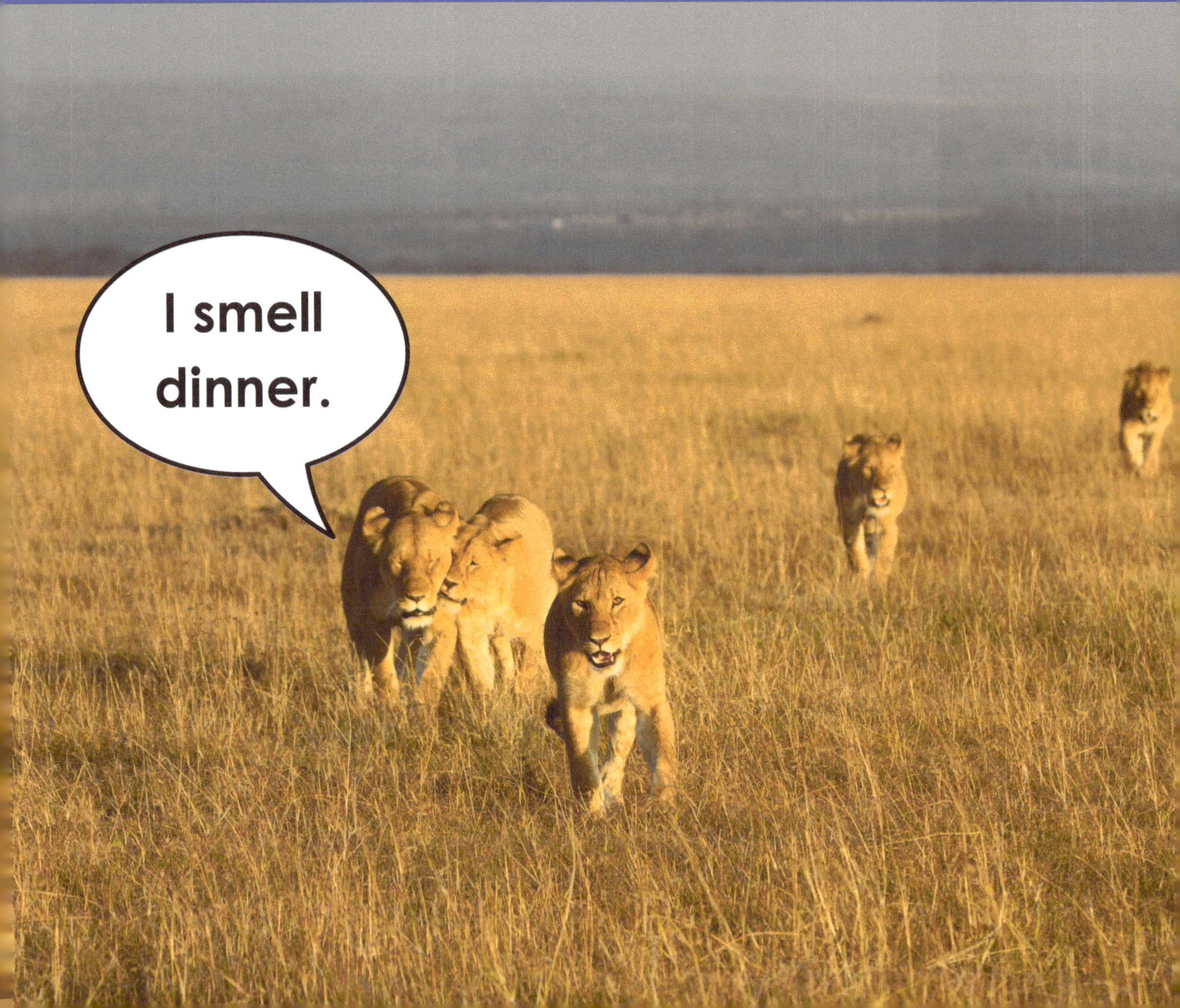

Lions have "retractable" claws.

I can put my claws away when I'm not using them.

We usually win...but not always.

In some places, lions may have to fight crocodiles or hyenas.

Lions communicate with each other through roars, growls, and even purrs.

Let's go out for dinner.

Sounds good.

A lion's roar can be heard from miles away.

Lions can run up to 50 m (80 km) per hour for short distances.

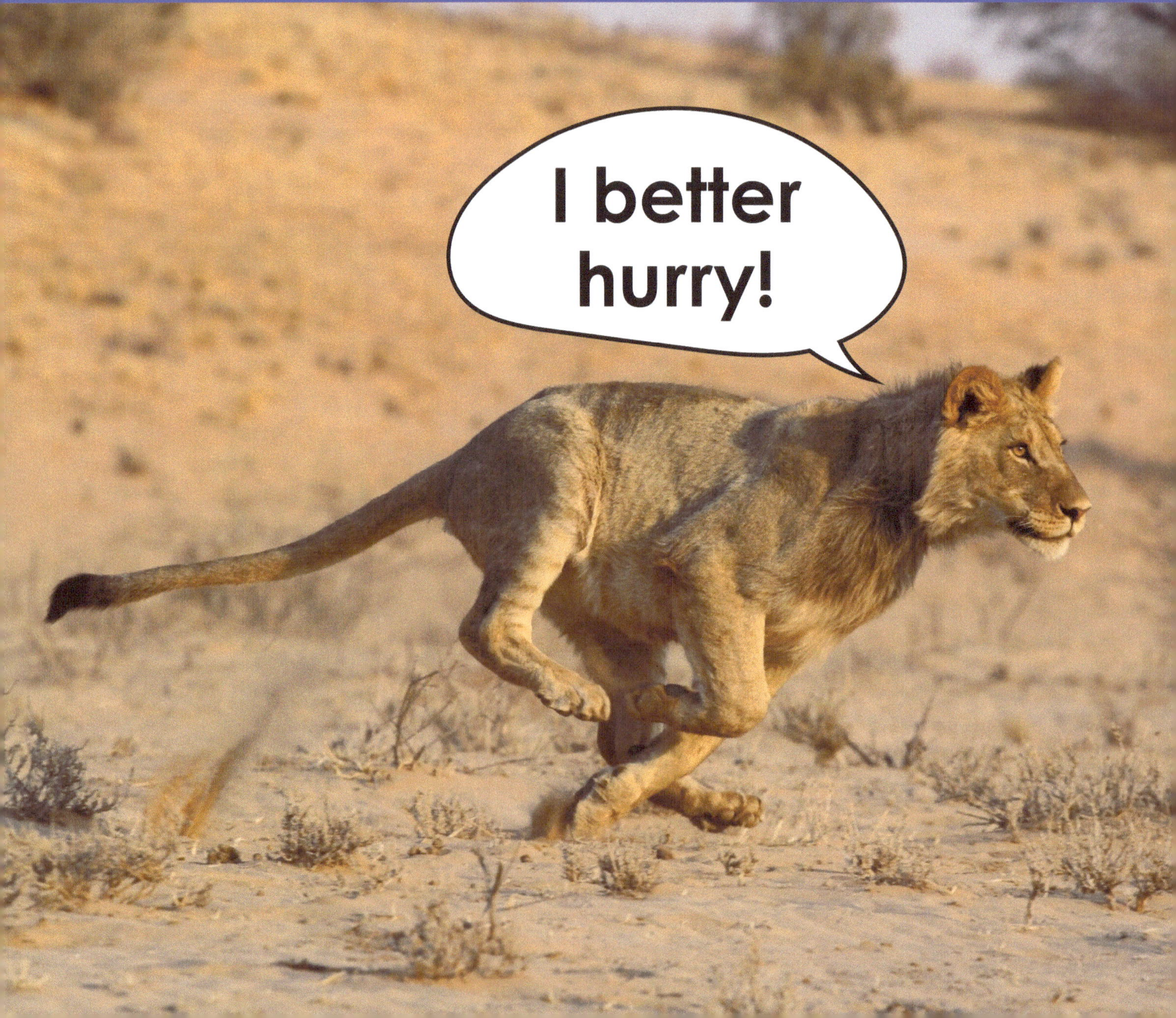

A group of lions is called a "pride".

This is the best napping spot.

A pride usually has related females and young lions.

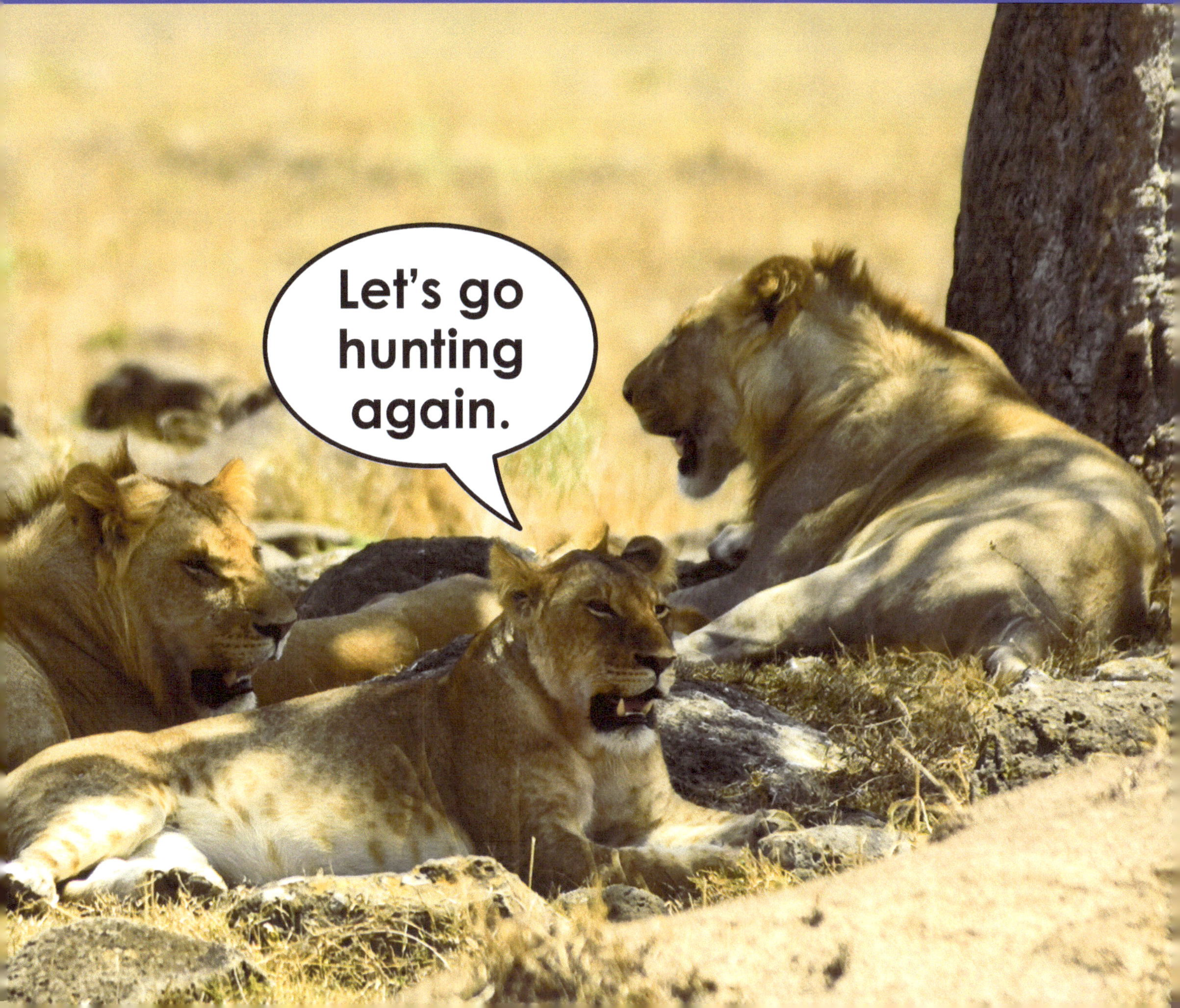

Baby lions are called "cubs".

There are usually 2-6 of us born to a litter.

Cubs are born with spots on their bodies.

Call me Spot!

Cubs learn to hunt by playing with each other.

I'm going to be a great hunter like mom!

No, I am!

Lioness moms are super caring.

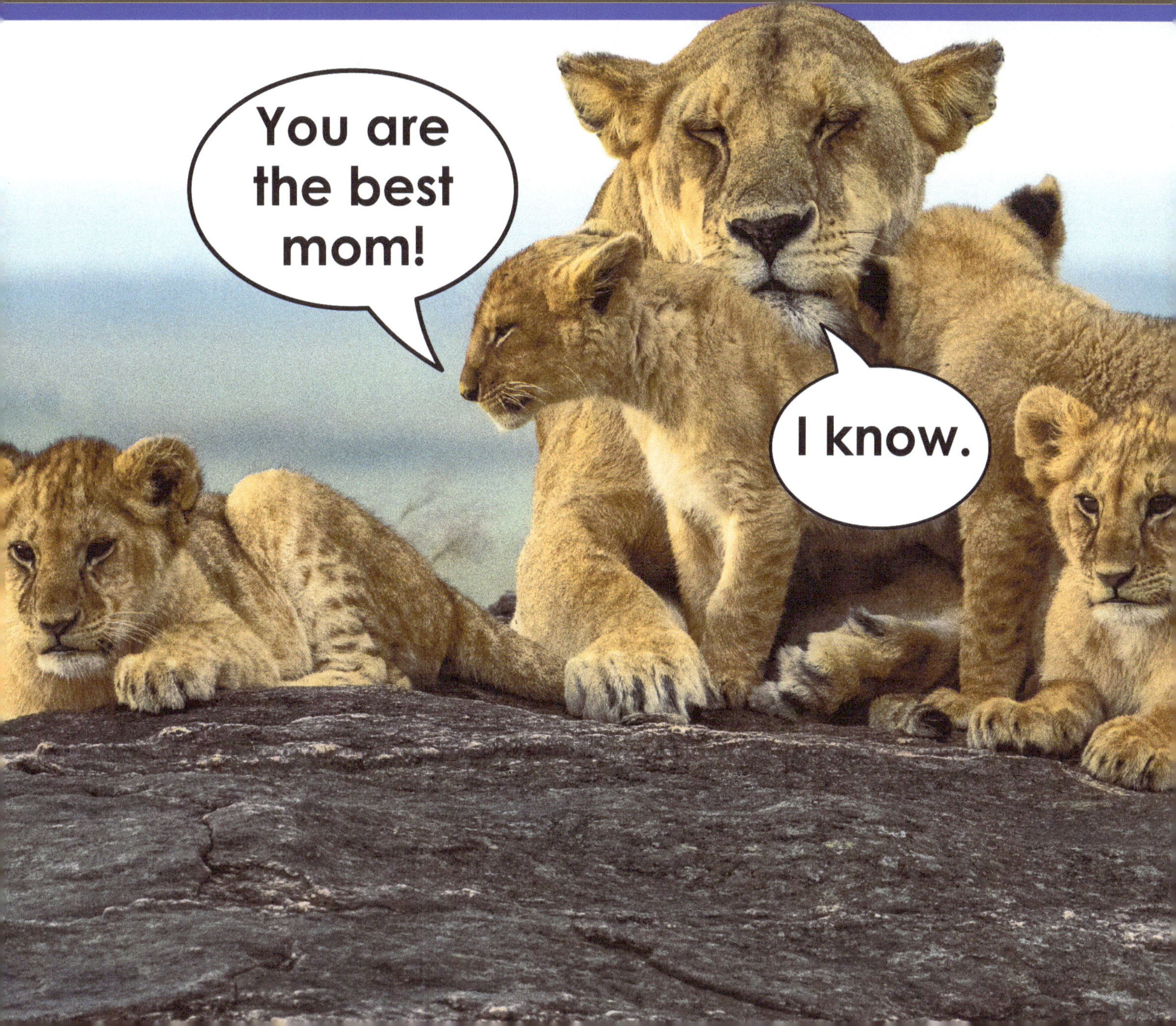

Lions are social animals.

Lions often show affection by grooming each other.

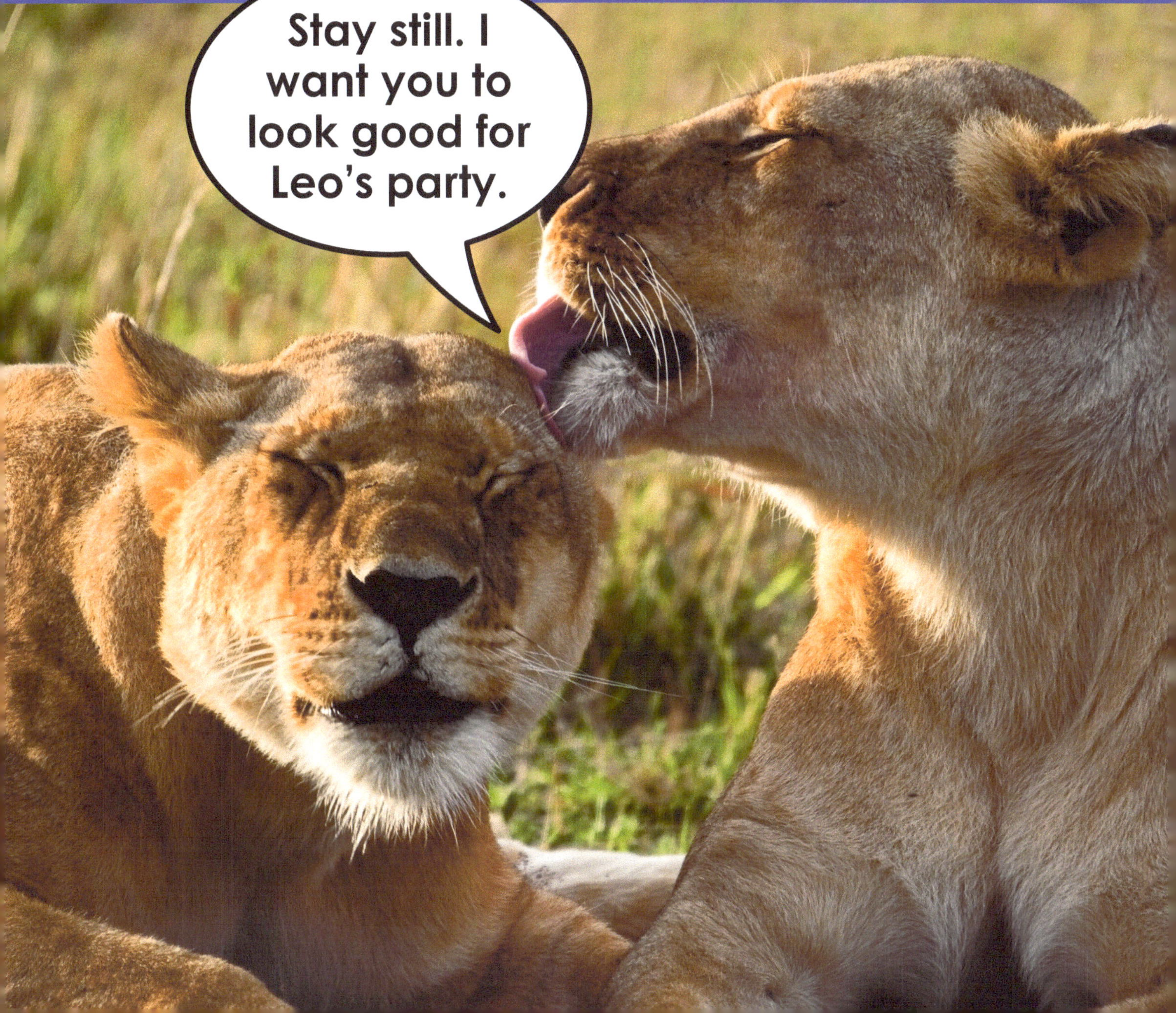

I am a lion. Goodbye!

Hello parents!

Visit us to find out about new releases and *FREE* offers. We'll let you know when we have a new release coming out and how you can get it for FREE.

And you can cast your vote for what book we make next!

scan here

or visit here

ActiveBrainsBooks.com

---

scan here

Let us know what you think. As an independent publisher, your honest reviews mean a lot to us and our business. We'd love to hear from you!

amazon.com/review/create-review/

or visit here

FOLLOW US on Amazon.

amazon.com/author/activebrainsbooks

ActiveBrainsBooks.com

ACTIVE BRAINS

www.ingramcontent.com/pod-product-compliance
Lightning Source LLC
Chambersburg PA
CBHW060844270326
41933CB00003B/189